Christmas Delights Journal
A Daily Journal

Hood Holiday Journal Series – Book 12

Karen Jean Matsko Hood

Christmas Delights Journal
A Daily Journal
Hood Holiday Journal Series – Book 12

Gift Inscription

To: _____

From: _____

Date: _____

Special Message: _____

_____

_____

_____

_____

_____

_____

_____

It is always nice to receive a personal note to create a special memory.

www.WhisperingPinePress.com
www.WhisperingPinePressBookstore.com

Christmas Delights Journal

A Daily Journal

Hood Holiday Journal Series – Book 12

Karen Jean Matsko Hood

Published by:

Whispering Pine Press International, Inc.
Your Northwest Book Publishing Company
2510 North Pines Road, Suite 206, Sales Room
Spokane Valley, WA 99206-7636 USA
Phone: (509) 928-7888 | Fax: (509) 922-9949
Email: sales@whisperingpinepress.com
Websites: www.WhisperingPinePress.com
www.WhisperingPinePressBookstore.com
Blog: www.WhisperingPinePressBlog.com
SAN 253-200X
Printed in the U.S.A.

Published by Whispering Pine Press International, Inc.
International Publishing Company
2510 North Pines Road, Suite 206, Sales Room
Spokane Valley, Washington 99206-7636 USA

Copyright © 2014 by Karen Jean Matsko Hood
All rights reserved.

No part of this publication may be reproduced, translated, stored in a retrieval system, or transmitted in any form by any means, including electronic, mechanical photocopying, recording, or otherwise without the prior written permission from the publisher, Whispering Pine Press International, Inc.

For sales outside the United States, please contact the Whispering Pine Press International, Inc., International Sales Department.

Manufactured in the United States of America. This paper is acid-free and 100% chlorine free.

Book and Cover Design by Artistic Design Service, Inc.
Spokane Valley, WA 99206-7636 USA
www.ArtisticDesignService.com

Library of Congress Number (LCCN): 2014916770

Hood, Karen Jean Matsko
  Title: Christmas Delights Journal: A Daily Journal, Hood Holiday Journal Series – Book 12

    p. cm.

ISBN: 978-1-59434-974-4	case bound
ISBN: 978-1-59434-501-2	perfect bound
ISBN: 978-1-59434-160-1	spiral bound
ISBN: 978-1-59434-975-1	E-PDF
ISBN: 978-1-59434-506-7	E-PUB
ISBN: 978-1-59434-161-8	E-PRC

First Edition: November 2014
1. Journal (*Christmas Delights Journal: A Daily Journal, Hood Journal Series – Book 12*)   1. Title

Christmas Delights Journal
A Daily Journal
Hood Holiday Journal Series – Book 12

Table of Contents

Title Page 1
Gift Inscription 2
Publisher Page 3
Copyright Page 4
Table of Contents 5
Journal Pages 6-144
Dedications 145
Acknowledgements 146
Praise 147-148
Reader Feedback Form 149
About the Cookbook Delights Series 150

Order Forms:
   Book Club 151
   Fundraising Opportunities 152
   Personalized and/or Translated Order Form 153
   Whispering Pine Press International, Inc.,
   Order Forms 154-156
Current and Future Books by the Author 157-158
About the Author and Cook 159-160

Did You Know? . . . .

Did you know the top Christmas tree producing states are Oregon, North Carolina, Michigan, Pennsylvania, Wisconsin, and Washington?

Did You Know? . . . .

Did you know there are about 500,000 acres in production for growing Christmas trees in the United States?

Did You Know? . . . .

Did you know our early holiday experiences shape our lifetime expectations of these special occasions? If you begin when your kids are very young to emphasize the religious, cultural, and altruistic traditions of Christmas, and if you de-emphasize the commercial hoopla, you will be giving them gifts that will last far longer than any toys that money can buy.

_____
_____
_____
_____
_____
_____
_____
_____
_____
_____
_____
_____

Did You Know? . . . .

Did you know that in 1939, an advertising employee at the department store Montgomery Ward wrote the story of Rudolph the Red-Nosed Reindeer for a store promotion? That year the store gave away 2.4 million copies of the story.

Did You Know? . . . .

Ten years later, Gene Autry recorded the song "Rudolph the Red-Nosed Reindeer." Since then it has sold over 80 million copies. Rudolph has definitely gone down in our holiday history.

Did You Know?....

Did you know that on Christmas Eve in 2001, the Bethlehem Hotel had 208 of its 210 rooms free?

Did You Know? . . . .

Did you know you can ensure a longer lasting Christmas tree by simply removing the bottom 2 inches of your tree trunk before placing the tree in the stand? This enables your tree to absorb water.

Did You Know? . . . .

Did you know you can ensure a longer lasting Christmas tree by never letting the water reservoir go dry?

Did You Know? . . . .

Did you know that the greater part of our happiness or our misery depends on our dispositions and not on our circumstances?

Did You Know? . . . .

Did you know who made that previous famous quote? ~ Martha Washington ~ Born June 21, 1732. A very wise lady.

Did You Know? . . . .

Did you know that in 1949, the tree at Rockefeller Center was strung with 7,500 bulbs? Now more than 25,000 bulbs are strung on the tree - that's more than 5 miles of lights.

Did You Know?....

Did you know that artificial Christmas trees were on the market by 1900? They were available by mail from Sears, Roebuck and Company, and cost 50 cents for 33 limbs, or a dollar for 55 limbs.

Did You Know? . . . .

Did you know that a national biscuit company introduced "Barnum's Animal Crackers" as a holiday promotion in 1902? The string-carrying boxes were designed for hanging on the Christmas tree.

Did You Know? . . . .

Did you know that North American real Christmas trees are grown in all 50 states and in Canada?

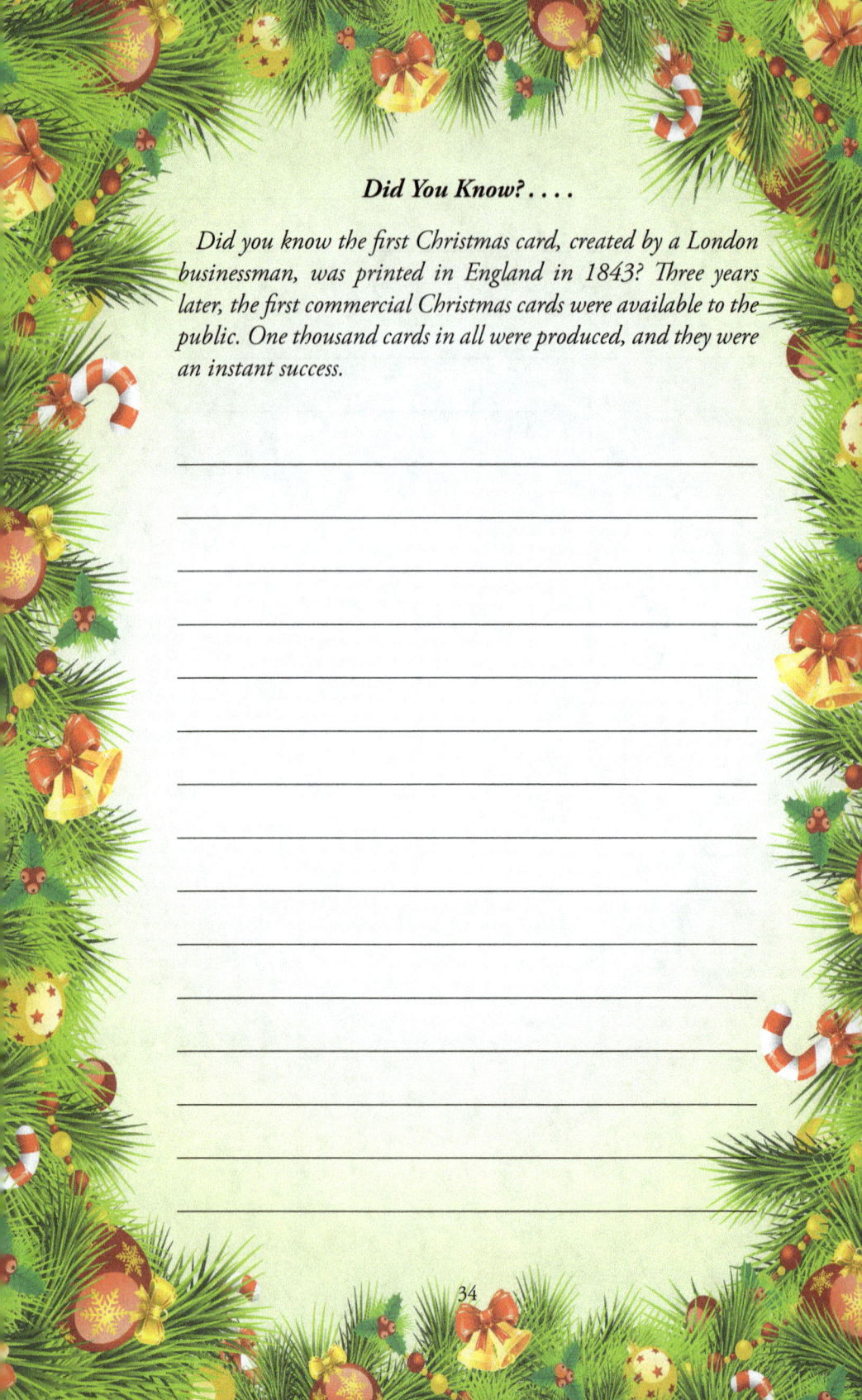

Did You Know?....

Did you know the first Christmas card, created by a London businessman, was printed in England in 1843? Three years later, the first commercial Christmas cards were available to the public. One thousand cards in all were produced, and they were an instant success.

Did You Know? . . . .

Did you know that it's the idea of giving that reminds us we are all on this planet together, for the long run? So let's be kind to one another.

Did You Know? . . . .

Did you know that an acre of Christmas trees produces the daily oxygen for 18 people?

Did You Know? . . . .

Did you know that for every real Christmas tree harvested, up to 3 seedlings are planted in its place the following spring?

Did You Know? . . . .

Did you know there are approximately 30 to 35 million real Christmas trees sold in the U.S. every year?

Did You Know? . . . .

Did you know that you can locate the nearest recycling program by logging onto www.realchristmastrees.org or calling 1-800-CLEANUP?

Did You Know? . . . .

Did you know that bells summoning the faithful to worship was the first link to Christmas?

Did You Know? . . . .

Did you know the most precious gift you can receive is sharing with someone the gift of giving?

Did You Know?....

Did you know that one of the greatest joys you will ever feel is the look in your child's eyes when he gives a plate of cookies you have made together to a neighbor or friend, or a stranger?

Did You Know? . . . .

Did you know the top selling Christmas trees are: balsam fir, Douglas fir, Fraser fir, noble fir, Scotch pine, Virginia pine, and white pine?

Did You Know? . . . .

Did you know that our custom of kissing under the mistletoe came from the beliefs of the Scandinavians that holly was a symbol of peace?

Did You Know? . . . .

Did you know that during Roman times, holly was a symbol of peace and good will?

Did You Know?....

Did you know in England, people used to believe holly brought good luck and served as protection from witches?

Did You Know? . . . .

Did you know there are about 21,000 Christmas tree growers in the United States, and over 100,000 people employed full or part-time in the industry?

_____
_____
_____
_____
_____
_____
_____
_____
_____
_____
_____
_____
_____
_____
_____

Did You Know? . . . .

Did you know Christmas caroling began as an old English custom called Wassailing - toasting neighbors to a long and healthy life?

_____
_____
_____
_____
_____
_____
_____
_____
_____
_____
_____
_____
_____
_____

Did You Know? . . . .

Did you know we kiss under the mistletoe because the ancient Norse associated mistletoe with their goddess of love?

Did You Know? . . . .

Did you know the growth of mistletoe is parasitic on trees?

Did You Know? . . . .

Did you know mistletoe in the Middle Ages was considered mysterious and even sacred?

Did You Know? . . . .

Did you know that in Spain children leave their shoes under the Christmas tree the night of January 5th and presents from the Three Kings (Los Reyes Magos: Melchor, Gaspar, and Baltasar) appear the next morning? Santa Claus is called Papa Noel and some children receive presents both days: on December 24th (from Papa Noel) and on January 6th (from the Three Kings).

Did You Know? . . . .

Did you know that in England, Christmas is rung in starting on December 21st?

Did You Know? . . . .

Did you know that during the holidays there are many good deeds waiting to be done by your child and you, together?

Did You Know? . . . .

Did you know one of the most precious gifts is time?

Did You Know? . . . .

Did you know another gift you can give your children is to engage them in cultural, religious, and traditional activities throughout the Christmas season?

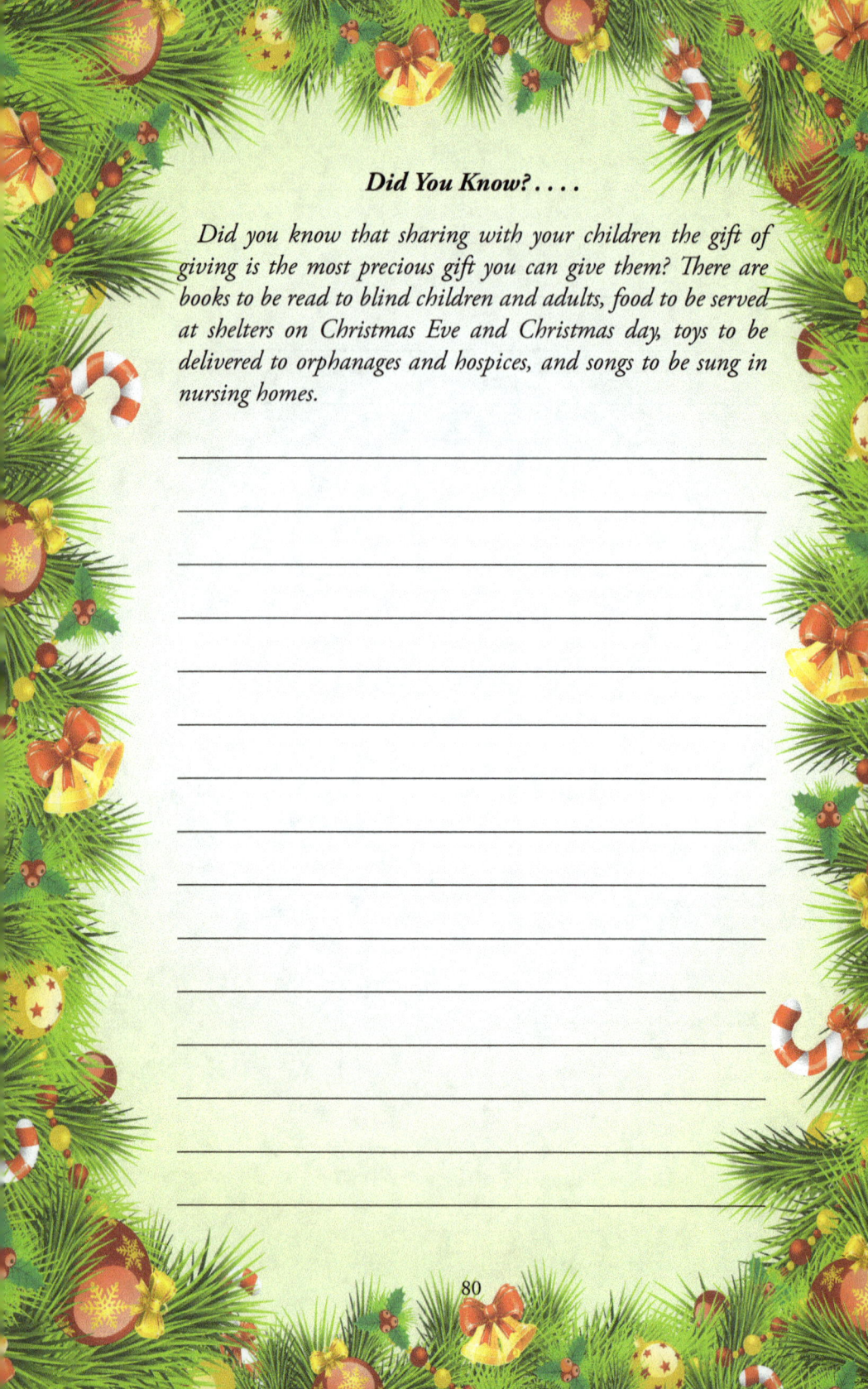

Did You Know?....

Did you know that sharing with your children the gift of giving is the most precious gift you can give them? There are books to be read to blind children and adults, food to be served at shelters on Christmas Eve and Christmas day, toys to be delivered to orphanages and hospices, and songs to be sung in nursing homes.

Did You Know?....

Did you know you can create family traditions that involve giving back to the community? Shopping for extra groceries to give to a food bank, volunteering at a shelter, or donating toys are all ways that even young children can get involved in to help others.

Did You Know? . . . .

Did you know that if you talk with your kids about the roots of your family's traditions, you share a deeper gift?

Did You Know? . . . .

Did you know a sparkle in a child's eyes is contagious?

Did You Know?....

Did you know the "Twelve Days of Christmas" refers to the time taken by the Three Wise Men (the Magi) to reach Bethlehem to see the babe in the manger, Jesus?

Did You Know? . . . .

Did you know that telling kids the religious story of Christmas at an early age, and retelling it as they grow, will help them remember the deeper meaning of the holiday?

Did You Know? . . . .

Did you know that if you don't have any castor sugar on hand, you can make your own by grinding granulated sugar for a couple of minutes in a food processor?

Did You Know? . . . .

Did you know that poinsettias are flowers found in the wild in deciduous tropical forests at moderate elevations from southern Sinaloa down the entire Pacific coast of Mexico to Chiapas and into Guatemala?

Did You Know? . . . .

Did you know that the tradition of a holiday tree has been around since ancient times and has played an important part in winter celebrations for many centuries?

Did You Know? . . . .

Did you know that few Americans, to be sure, bother with a Yule log any longer; yet the Yule log was once one of the most firmly entrenched of customs?

Did You Know?....

Did you know that the story of Christmas begins with the birth of a baby in Bethlehem? It is believed that Christ was born on the 25th, although the exact month is unknown.

Did You Know? . . . .

Did you know that the pure green color of the stately fir tree remains green all year round, depicting the everlasting hope of mankind? All the needles point toward heaven, making it a symbol of man's thoughts turning toward heaven.

Did You Know?....

Did you know that many Christmas practices originate in Germanic countries, including the Christmas tree, the Christmas ham, the Yule log, holly, mistletoe, and the giving of presents?

Did You Know? . . . .

Did you know that there are exactly 109 varieties of poinsettias available, but 69 percent of Americans still prefer red poinsettias, 7 percent prefer white, and 14 percent prefer pink?

Did You Know? . . . .

Did you know that in 1841 the English royalty helped popularize the tree in England by decorating the first Christmas tree at Windsor Castle?

Did You Know? . . . .

Did you know that often a stump or root, it was brought home Christmas Eve, where it was placed in the kitchen hearth or in the main fireplace?

Did You Know? . . . .

Did you know that it was in 350 A.D. that December 25 was declared the official date for celebrating Christmas by Pope Julius I?

Did You Know? . . . .

Did you know that the star was the heavenly sign of promises long ago? God promised a Savior for the world, and the star was the sign of fulfillment of His promise.

Did You Know?....

Did you know that in the southern hemisphere, Christmas is during the summer? This clashes with the traditional winter iconography, resulting in oddities such as a red fur-coated Santa Claus surfing in for a turkey barbecue.

_____
_____
_____
_____
_____
_____
_____
_____
_____
_____
_____
_____
_____
_____
_____
_____
_____
_____
_____
_____

Did You Know? . . . .

Did you know that poinsettias are named after Joel Roberts Poinsett, the first United States ambassador to Mexico, who introduced the plant in the United States in 1825?

Did You Know? . . . .

Did you know that to protect your poinsettia from chilling winds when transporting plants, carry them in a large shopping bag?

Did You Know? . . . .

Did you know that the colors most often associated with Christmas decorating are green, red, white, blue, silver, and gold? These colors have been used for centuries and, as with most traditions, the reason may be traced to religious beliefs.

Did You Know?....

Did you know that the candle symbolizes that Christ is the light of the world, and when we see this great light we are reminded of He who displaces the darkness?

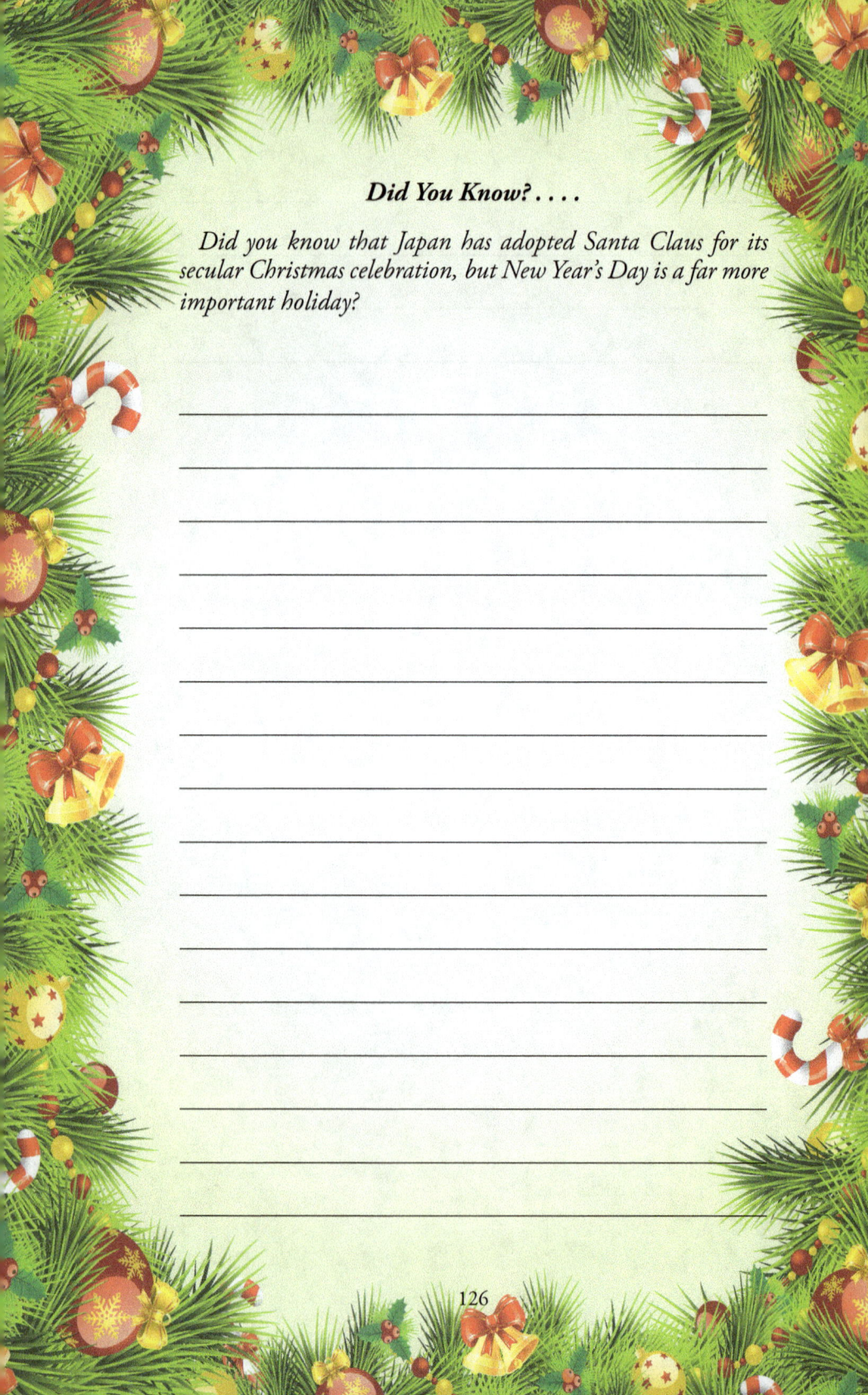

Did You Know? . . . .

Did you know that Japan has adopted Santa Claus for its secular Christmas celebration, but New Year's Day is a far more important holiday?

Did You Know? . . . .

Did you know that poinsettias need light, so place them in a bright place for at least six hours a day?

Did You Know? . . . .

Did you know that in 1914 there was a truce between German and British troops in France? Soldiers on both sides spontaneously began to sing Christmas carols and stopped fighting.

Did You Know? . . . .

Did you know that the wreath symbolizes the real nature of love? Real love never ceases. Love is one continuous round of affection.

Did You Know? . . . .

Did you know that Santa Claus symbolizes the generosity and good will we feel during the month of December?

Did You Know?....

Did you know that the holly plant represents immortality and the crown of thorns worn by our Savior? The red holly berries represent the blood shed by Him.

Did You Know? . . . .

Did you know that God so loved the world that He gave His only begotten Son? Thanks be to God for his unspeakable gift.

Did You Know? . . . .

Did you know that the wise men bowed before the Holy Babe and presented Him with gold, frankincense, and myrrh? We should always give gifts in the same spirit of the wise men.

_____
_____
_____
_____
_____
_____
_____
_____
_____
_____
_____
_____
_____
_____
_____

Did You Know?....

Did you know that the candy cane represents the shepherds' crook? The crook on the staff helps to bring back strayed sheep to the flock. The candy cane is the symbol that we are our brother's keeper.

Did You Know? . . . .

Did you know that the angels heralded the glorious news of the Savior's birth? The angels sang glory to God in the highest, on earth peace and good will toward men.

Dedications

To my husband and best friend, Jim.

To our seventeen children: Gabriel, Brianne Kristina and her husband Moulik Vinodkumar Kothari, Marissa Kimberly and her husband Kevin Matthew Franck, Janelle Karina and her husband Paul Joseph Turcotte, Mikayla Karlene, Kyler James, Kelsey Katrina, Corbin Joel, Caleb Jerome, Keisha Kalani Hiwot, Devontay Joshua, Kianna Karielle Selam, Rosy Kiara, Mercedes Katherine, Jasmine Khalia Wengel, Cheyenne Krystal, and Annalise Kaylee Marie.

To Nola Paige, Zoey Karina, and future grandchildren.

To our foster grandchildren: Courtney, Lorenzo, and Leah.

To my brother, Stephen, and his wife, Karen.

To my husband's ten siblings: Gary, Colleen, John, Dan, Mary, Ray, Ann, Teresa, Barbara, Agnes, and their families.

In loving memory of my mom, who passed away in 2007; my dad, who passed away in 1976; and my sister, Sandy, who passed away due to multiple sclerosis in 1999.

To Sandy's three sons: Monte, Bradley, and Derek. To Monte's wife, Sarah, and their children: Liam, Alice, Charlie, Samuel and their foster children. To Bradley's wife, Shawnda, and their children: Anton, Isaac, and Isabel.

To our foster children past and present: Krystal, Sara, Rebecca, Janice, Devontay Joshua, Mercedes Katherine, Zha'Nell, Makia, Onna, Cheyenne Krystal, Onna Marie, Nevaeh, and Zada, our future foster children, and all foster children everywhere.

To the Court Appointed Special Advocate (CASA) Volunteer Program in the judicial system which benefits abused and neglected children.

To the Literacy Campaign dedicated to promoting literacy throughout the world.

Acknowledgements

The author would like to acknowledge all those individuals who helped me during my time in writing this book. Appreciation is extended for all their support and effort they put into this project.

Deep gratitude and profound thanks are owed to my husband, Jim, for giving freely of his time and encouragement during this project.

Also, thanks are owed to my children Gabriel, Brianne Kristina and her husband Moulik Vinodkumar Kothari, Marissa Kimberly and her husband Kevin Matthew Franck, Janelle Karina and her husband Paul Joseph Turcotte, Mikayla Karlene, Kyler James, Kelsey Katrina, Corbin Joel, Caleb Jerome, Keisha Kalani Hiwot, Devontay Joshua, Kianna Karielle Selam, Rosy Kiara, Mercedes Katherine, Jasmine Khalia Wengel, Cheyenne Krystal, and Annalise Kaylee Marie. All of these persons inspire my writing.

Thanks are due to Pam Alexandrovich and Sharron Thompson for their assistance in editing and typing this manuscript for publication. Thanks go to Artistic Design Service, Inc. for their assistance in formatting and providing a graphic design of this manuscript for publication. This project could not have been completed without them.

Many thanks are due to members of my family, all of whom were very supportive during the time it took to complete this project. Their patience and support are greatly appreciated.

Praise for Christmas Delights Journal
A Daily Journal
Hood Holiday Journal Series – Book 12

…"Each year I like to search for fun, new, and creative ways to surprise my family on Christmas Day. Since discovering **Christmas Delights Journal**, I've been able to record my memories.

There are many ideas in this journal to help you show your children and friends just how much they mean to you. Treat yourself or someone you love to a copy of this journal today!"…

Kimberly Carter
Assistant

…"**Christmas Delights Journal** has blank pages for you to write your own notes or recipes.

Christmas Delights Journal will soon be part of your treasured collection of splendid holiday records to be passed down to future generations."…

Mary Scripture-Smith
Graphic Designer

Praise for Christmas Delights Journal
A Daily Journal
Hood Holiday Journal Series – Book 12

…"Whispering Pine Press International has done it again with the newest in their Cookbook Delights Holiday Series collection. **Christmas Delights Journal** continues the legacy of high quality work and craftsmanship from its author. The journal pages are designed to leave space to write your own journal notes and favorite recipes."…

Allyson Schnabel
Editor, Teacher

…"**Christmas Delights Journal** is a companion to Christmas Delights Cookbook. It gives you space to write your own journal notes or your favorite recipes."…

Ed Archambeault
Spokane, WA.

Reader Feedback Form

Dear Reader,

We are very interested in what our readers think. Please fill in the form below and return to:

Whispering Pine Press International, Inc.
International Publishing Company
c/o Christmas Delights Journal: A Daily Journal
2510 North Pines Road, Suite 206, Sales Room
Spokane Valley, WA 99206-7636
Phone: (509) 928-7888 | Fax: (509) 922-9949
Email: sales@whisperingpinepress.com
Publisher Websites: www.WhisperingPinePress.com
www.WhisperingPinePressBookstore.com
Blog: www.WhisperingPinePressBlog.com

Name: _____

Address: _____

City, St., Zip: _____

Phone/Fax: (___) _____ | (___) _____

Email: _____

Comments/Suggestions: _____

_____

_____

_____

_____

A great deal of care and attention has been exercised in the creation of this book. Designing a great cookbook that is original, fun, and easy to use has been a job that required many hours of diligence, creativity, and research. Although we strive to make this book completely error free, errors and discrepancies may not be completely excluded. If you come across any errors or discrepancies, please make a note of them and send them to our publishing office. We are constantly updating our manuscripts, eliminating errors, and improving quality.

Please contact us at the address above.

About the Cookbook Delights Series

The *Cookbook Delights Series* includes many different topics and themes. If you have a passion for food and wish to know more information about different foods, then this series of cookbooks will be beneficial to you. Each book features a different type of food, such as avocados, strawberries, huckleberries, salmon, vegetarian, lentils, almonds, cherries, coconuts, lemons, and many, many more.

The *Cookbook Delights Series* not only includes cookbooks about individual foods but also includes several holiday-themed cookbooks. Whatever your favorite holiday may be, chances are we have a cookbook with recipes designed with that holiday in mind. Some examples include *Halloween Delights, Thanksgiving Delights, Christmas Delights, Valentine Delights, Mother's Day Delights, St. Patrick's Day Delights,* and *Easter Delights.*

Each cookbook is designed for easy use and is organized into alphabetical sections. Over 250 recipes are included along with other interesting facts, folklore, and history of the featured food or theme. Each book comes with a beautiful full-color cover, ordering information, and a list of other upcoming books in the series.

Note cards, bookmarks, and a daily journal have been printed and are available to go along with each cookbook. You may view the entire line of cookbooks, journals, cards, posters, puzzles, and bookmarks by visiting our website at www.whisperingpinepress.com, or you can email us with your questions and your comments to: sales@whisperingpinepress.com.

Please ask your local bookstore to carry these sets of books.

To order, please contact:

Whispering Pine Press International, Inc.
International Publishing Company
c/o Christmas Delights Journal: A Daily Journal
2510 North Pines Road, Suite 206, Sales Room
Spokane Valley, WA 99206-7636
Phone: (509) 928-7888 | Fax: (509) 922-9949
Email: sales@whisperingpinepress.com
Publisher Websites: www.WhisperingPinePress.com
www.WhisperingPinePressBookstore.com
Blog: www.WhisperingPinePressBlog.com
SAN 253-200X

We Invite You to Join the Whispering Pine Press International, Inc. Book Club!

Whispering Pine Press International, Inc.
International Publishing Company
c/o Christmas Delights Journal: A Daily Journal
2510 North Pines Road, Suite 206, Sales Room
Spokane Valley, WA 99206-7636
Phone: (509) 928-7888 | Fax: (509) 922-9949
Email: sales@whisperingpinepress.com
Publisher Websites: www.WhisperingPinePress.com
www.WhisperingPinePressBookstore.com
Blog: www.WhisperingPinePressBlog.com

Buy 11 books and get the next one free, based on the average price of the first eleven purchased.

How the club works:
Simply use the order form below and order books from our catalog. You can buy just one at a time or all eleven at once. After the first eleven books are purchased, the next one is free. Please add shipping and handling as listed on this form. There are no purchase requirements at any time during your membership. Free book credit is based on the average price of the first eleven books purchased.

Join today! Pick your books and mail in the form today!
Yes! I want to join the Whispering Pine Press International, Inc., Book Club! Enroll me and send the books indicated below.

Title   Price
1. _____
2. _____
3. _____
4. _____
5. _____
6. _____
7. _____
8. _____
9. _____
10. _____
11. _____
Free Book Title: _____
Free Book Price: _____ Avg. Price: _____ Total Price: _____
    Credit for the free book is based on the average price of the first 11 books purchased.
    (Circle one) Check | Visa | MasterCard | Discover | American Express
Credit Card #: _____ Expiration Date: _____
Name: _____
Address: _____
City: _____ State: _____ Country: _____
Zip/Postal: _____ Phone: (_____) _____
Email: _____
Signature _____

Whispering Pine Press International, Inc. Fundraising Opportunities

Fundraising cookbooks are proven moneymakers and great keepsake providers for your group. Whispering Pine Press International, Inc., offers a very special personalized cookbook fundraising program that encourages success to organizations all across the USA.

Our prices are competitive and fair. Currently, we offer a special of 100 books with many free features and excellent customer service. Any purchase you make is guaranteed first-rate.

Flexibility is not a problem. If you have special needs, we guarantee our cooperation in meeting each of them. Our goal is to create a cookbook that goes beyond your expectations. We have the confidence and a record that promises continual success.

Another great fundraising program is the *Cookbook Delights Series* Program. With cookbook orders of 50 copies or more, your organization receives a huge discount, making for a prompt and lucrative solution.

We also specialize in assisting group fundraising – Christian, community, nonprofit, and academic among them. If you are struggling for a new idea, something that will enhance your success and broaden your appeal, Whispering Pine Press International, Inc., can help.

For more information, write, phone, or fax to:

Whispering Pine Press International, Inc.
International Publishing Company
2510 North Pines Road, Suite 206, Sales Room
Spokane Valley, WA 99206-7636
Phone: (509) 928-7888 | Fax: (509) 922-9949
Email: sales@whisperingpinepress.com
Publisher Websites: www.WhisperingPinePress.com
www.WhisperingPinePressBookstore.com
Blog: www.WhisperingPinePressBlog.com

SAN 253-200X

Personalized and/or Translated Order Form for Any Book by Whispering Pine Press International, Inc.

Dear Readers:

If you or your organization wishes to have this book or any other of our books personalized, we will gladly accommodate your needs. For instance, if you would like to change the names of the characters in a book to the names of the children in your family or Sunday school class, we would be happy to work with you on such a project. We can add more information of your choosing and customize this book especially for your family, group, or organization.

We are also offering an option of translating your book into another language. Please fill out the form below telling us exactly how you would like us to personalize your book.

Please send your request to:

Whispering Pine Press International, Inc.
International Publishing Company
c/o Christmas Delights Journal: A Daily Journal
2510 North Pines Road, Suite 206, Sales Room
Spokane Valley, WA 99206-7636
Phone: (509) 928-7888 | Fax: (509) 922-9949
Email: sales@whisperingpinepress.com
Publisher Websites: www.WhisperingPinePress.com
www.WhisperingPinePressBookstore.com
Blog: www.WhisperingPinePressBlog.com

Person/Organization placing request: _____

_____Date: _____

Phone: (___) _____ Fax: (___) _____

Address: _____

City: _____ State: _____ Zip: _____

Language of the book: _____

Please explain your request in detail: _____

_____

_____

_____

Christmas Delights Journal
A Daily Journal
Hood Holiday Journal Series – Book 12
How to Order

Get your additional copies of this book by returning an order form and your check, money order, or credit card information to:

Whispering Pine Press International, Inc.
International Publishing Company
c/o Christmas Delights Journal: A Daily Journal
2510 North Pines Road, Suite 206, Sales Room
Spokane Valley, WA 99206-7636
Phone: (509) 928-7888 | Fax: (509) 922-9949
Email: sales@whisperingpinepress.com
Publisher Websites: www.WhisperingPinePress.com
www.WhisperingPinePressBookstore.com
Blog: www.WhisperingPinePressBlog.com

Customer Name: _____

Address: _____

City, St., Zip: _____

Phone/Fax: _____

Email: _____

- -

Please send me _____ copies of _____ _____

_____ at $_____ per copy and $5.95 for shipping and handling per book, plus $3.95 each for additional books. Enclosed is my check, money order, or charge my account for $_____.

☐ Check ☐ Money Order ☐ Credit Card

(*Circle One*) MasterCard | Discover | Visa | American Express
☐☐☐☐   ☐☐☐☐   ☐☐☐☐   ☐☐☐☐

Expiration Date: _____

_____
Signature

_____
Print Name

Whispering Pine Press International, Inc. Order Form

Gift-wrapping, Autographing, and Inscription

We are proud to offer personal autographing by the author. For a limited time this service is absolutely free! Gift-wrapping is also available for $4.95 per item.

1. Sold To
Name: _____
Street/Route: _____
_____
City: _____
State: _____ Zip: _____
Country: _____
Gift message: _____
_____
Email address: _____
Daytime Phone: (___) ___-____
*Necessary for verifying orders
Home Phone: (___) ___-____
Fax: (___) ___-____

2. Ship To
☐ Is this a new or corrected address?
☐ Alternative Shipping Address
☐ Mailing Address
Name: _____
Address: _____
_____
City: _____
State: _____ Zip: _____
Country: _____
Email address: _____

3. Items Ordered

ISBN # /Item #	Size	Color	Qty.	Title or Description	Price	Total

4. Method Of Payment
International, Inc. (No Cash or COD's)

☐ Visa ☐ MasterCard ☐ Discover ☐ American Express ☐ Check/Money Order
Please make it payable to Whispering Pine Press International, Inc. (No Cash or COD's)

Account Number   Expiration Date
                            ____ / ____
                            Month Year

☐☐☐☐ ☐☐☐☐ ☐☐☐☐ ☐☐☐☐

Signature_____
          Cardholder's signature
Printed Name_____
          Please print name of cardholder
Address of Cardholder_____

Subtotal	
Gift wrap $4.95 Each	
For delivery in WA add 8.7% sales tax.	
Shipping See chart at left	
6. Total	

5. Shipping & Handling

Continental US
US Postal Ground: For books please add $4.95 for the first book and $2.95 each for additional books.
All non-book items, add 15% of the Subtotal.
Please allow 1-4 weeks for delivery.
US Postal Air: Please add $15.00 shipping and handling.
Please allow 1-3 days for delivery.
Alaska, Hawaii, and the US Territories By Ship:
Please add 10% shipping and handling (minimum charge $15.00).

Please
By Air: Please add 12% shipping and handling (minimum charge $15.00).
Please allow 2-6 weeks for delivery.
International By Ship: Please add 10% shipping and handling (minimum charge $15.00).
Please allow 6-12 weeks for delivery.
By Air: Please add 12% shipping and handling (minimum charge $15.00).
Please allow 2-6 weeks for delivery.
FedEx Shipments: Add $5.00 to the above airmail charges for overnight delivery.

Shop Online:
www.WhisperingPinePress.com
Fax orders to: (509) 922-9949

Whispering Pine Press International, Inc.
2510 North Pines Road, Suite 206, Sales Room
Spokane Valley, WA 99206-7636 USA
Phone: (509) 928-7888 • Fax: (509) 922-9949
Email: sales@whisperingpinepress.com
Website: www.WhisperingPinePress.com

Whispering Pine Press International, Inc. Order Form

Gift-wrapping, Autographing, and Inscription
We are proud to offer personal autographing by the author. For a limited time this service is absolutely free! Gift-wrapping is also available for $4.95 per item.

1. Sold To
Name: _____
Street/Route: _____
_____
City: _____
State: _____ Zip: _____
Country: _____
Gift message: _____
_____

Email address: _____
Daytime Phone: (_ _ _) _ _ _-_ _ _ _
*Necessary for verifying orders
Home Phone: (_ _ _) _ _ _-_ _ _ _
Fax: (_ _ _) _ _ _-_ _ _ _

2. Ship To
☐ Is this a new or corrected address?
☐ Alternative Shipping Address
☐ Mailing Address
Name: _____
Address: _____
_____
City: _____
State: _____ Zip: _____
Country: _____
Email address: _____

3. Items Ordered

ISBN # /Item #	Size	Color	Qty.	Title or Description	Price	Total

4. Method Of Payment
International, Inc. (No Cash or COD's)

☐ Visa ☐ MasterCard ☐ Discover ☐ American Express ☐ Check/Money Order
Please make it payable to Whispering Pine Press International, Inc. (No Cash or COD's)

Account Number   Expiration Date
                                    ___ / ___
                                    Month Year
☐☐☐☐ ☐☐☐☐ ☐☐☐☐ ☐☐☐☐

Signature_____
              Cardholder's signature
Printed Name_____
              Please print name of cardholder
Address of Cardholder_____

Subtotal	
Gift wrap $4.95 Each	
For delivery in WA add 8.7% sales tax.	
Shipping See chart at left	
6. Total	

5. Shipping & Handling

Continental US
US Postal Ground: For books please add $4.95 for the first book and $2.95 each for additional books.
All non-book items, add 15% of the Subtotal.
Please allow 1-4 weeks for delivery.
US Postal Air: Please add $15.00 shipping and handling.
Please allow 1-3 days for delivery.
Alaska, Hawaii, and the US Territories By Ship:
Please add 10% shipping and handling
(minimum charge $15.00).

Please
By Air: Please add 12% shipping and handling (minimum charge $15.00).
Please allow 2-6 weeks for delivery.
International By Ship: Please add 10% shipping and handling (minimum charge $15.00).
Please allow 6-12 weeks for delivery.
By Air: Please add 12% shipping and handling (minimum charge $15.00).
Please allow 2-6 weeks for delivery.
FedEx Shipments: Add $5.00 to the above airmail charges for overnight delivery.

Shop Online:
www.WhisperingPinePress.com
Fax orders to: (509) 922-9949

Whispering Pine Press International, Inc.
2510 North Pines Road, Suite 206, Sales Room
Spokane Valley, WA 99206-7636 USA
Phone: (509) 928-7888 • Fax: (509) 922-9949
Email: sales@whisperingpinepress.com
Website: www.WhisperingPinePress.com

CURRENT AND FUTURE BOOKS FOR ADULTS
by Karen Jean Matsko Hood

Hood Holiday Journal Series

New Years Delights Journal – Book 1
Valentine Delights Journal – Book 2
St. Patrick's Day Delights Journal – Book 3
Easter Delights Journal – Book 4
Mother's Day Delights Journal – Book 5
Memorial Day Delights Journal – Book 6
Father's Day Delights Journal – Book 7
Fourth of July Delights Journal – Book 8
Labor Day Delights Journal – Book 9
Halloween Delights Journal – Book 10
Thanksgiving Delights Journal – Book 11
Christmas Delights Journal – Book 12

Hood Journal Series

Apple Delights Journal – Book 1
Blueberry Delights – Book 2
Chocolate Delights Journal – Book 3
Grape Delights Journal – Book 4
Huckleberry Delights Journal – Book 5
Lentil Delights Journal – Book 6
Onion Delights Journal – Book 7
Peach Delights Journal – Book 8
Pear Delights Journal – Book 9
Plum Delights Journal – Book 10
Prickly Pear Delights Journal – Book 11
Pumpkin Delights Journal – Book 12
Raspberry Delights Journal – Book 13
Rhubarb Delights Journal – Book 14
Strawberry Delights Journal – Book 15
Tea Time Delights Journal – Book 16
Wine Delights Journal – Book 17
Winemaking Delights Journal – Book 18

Cookbooks

Cookbook Delights Series

Apple Delights – Book 1
Blueberry Delights – Book 2
Chocolate Delights – Book 3
Grape Delights – Book 4
Huckleberry Delights – Book 5
Lentil Delights – Book 6
Onion Delights – Book 7
Peach Delights – Book 8
Pear Delights – Book 9
Plum Delights – Book 10
Prickly Pear Delights – Book 11
Pumpkin Delights – Book 12
Raspberry Delights – Book 13
Rhubarb Delights – Book 14
Strawberry Delights – Book 15
Tea Time Delights – Book 16
Wine Delights – Book 17
Winemaking Delights – Book 18

Cookbook Delights Holiday Series

New Years Delights – Book 1
Valentine Delights – Book 2
St. Patrick's Day Delights – Book 3
Easter Delights – Book 4
Mother's Day Delights - Book 5
Memorial Day Delights – Book 6
Father's Day Delights – Book 7
Fourth of July Delights – Book 8
Labor Day Delights – Book 9
Halloween Delights – Book 10
Thanksgiving Delights – Book 11
Christmas Delights – Book 12

Many of the above listed books are also available in bilingual and translated versions. Please contact Whispering Pine Press International, Inc., for details. This list of books is not all-inclusive.
For a complete list please visit our website or contact us at:

Whispering Pine Press International, Inc.
Your Northwest Book Publishing Company
2510 North Pines Road, Suite 206, Sales Room
Spokane Valley, WA 99206-7636 USA
Phone: (509) 928-7888 | Fax: (509) 922-9949
Email: sales@whisperingpinepress.com

Publisher Websites
Main Website: WhisperingPinePress.com
Online Store: WhisperingPinePressBookstore.com
WordPress Blogs: WhisperingPinePressBlog.com
WhisperingPinePressKidsBooks.com
WhisperingPinePressTeenBooks.com
WhisperingPinePressPoetry.com

Author Websites
Karen Jean Matsko Hood
Author Website: KarenJeanMatskoHood.com
Online Store: KarenJeanMatskoHoodBookstore.com
Author Blog: KarenJeanMatskoHoodBlog.com
Kids Books: KarensKidsBooks.com
KarensTeensBooks.com

Author's Social Media
Friend her on **Facebook**: Karen Jean Matsko Hood Author Fan Page
Please Follow the Author on **Twitter**: @KarenJeanHood
Google Plus Profile: Karen Jean Matsko Hood
Pinterest.com/KarenJMHood

About the Author and Cook

Karen Jean Matsko Hood has always enjoyed cooking, baking, and experimenting with recipes. At this time Hood is working to complete a series of cookbooks that blends her skills and experience in cooking and entertaining. Hood entertains large groups of people and especially enjoys designing creative menus with holiday, international, ethnic, and regional themes.

Hood is publishing a cookbook series entitled the *Cookbook Delights Series*, in which each cookbook emphasizes a different food ingredient or theme. The first cookbook in the series is *Apple Delights Cookbook*. Hood is working to complete another series of cookbooks titled *Hood and Matsko Family Cookbooks*, which includes many recipes handed down from her family heritage and others that have emerged from more current family traditions. She has been invited to speak on talk radio shows on various topics, and favorite recipes from her cookbooks have been prepared on local television programs.

Hood was born and raised in Great Falls, Montana. As an undergraduate, she attended the College of St. Benedict in St. Joseph, Minnesota, and St. John's University in Collegeville, Minnesota. She attended the University of Great Falls in Great Falls, Montana. Hood received a B.S. Degree in Natural Science from the College of St. Benedict and minored in both Psychology and Secondary Education. Upon her graduation, Hood and her husband taught science and math on the island of St. Croix in the U.S. Virgin Islands. Hood has completed postgraduate classes at the University of Iowa in Iowa City, Iowa. In May 2001, she completed her Master's Degree in Pastoral Ministry at Gonzaga University in Spokane, Washington. She has taken postgraduate classes at Lewis and Clark College on the North Idaho college campus in Coeur d'Alene, Idaho, Taylor University in Fort Wayne, Indiana, Spokane Falls Community College, Spokane Community College, Washington State University, University of Washington, and Eastern Washington University. Hood is working on research projects to complete her Ph.D. in Leadership Studies at Gonzaga University in Spokane, Washington.

Hood resides in Spokane, Washington, along with her husband, many of her sixteen children, and foster children. Her interests include writing, research, and teaching. She previously has volunteered as a court advocate in the Spokane juvenile court system for abused and neglected children. Hood is a literary advocate for youth and adults. Her hobbies include cooking, baking, collecting, photography, indoor and outdoor gardening, farming, and the cultivation of unusual flowering plants and orchids. She enjoys raising several specialty breeds of animals including Babydoll Southdown, Friesen, and Icelandic sheep, Icelandic and Arabian horses, Shetland pony, a variety of

Nubian and fainting goats, many breeds of chickens, ducks, geese, and other poultry, a few rescue cats, bichons frisés, cockapoos, Icelandic sheepdogs, a Newfoundland, a Rottweiler, and poodle dogs. Hood also enjoys bird-watching and finds all aspects of nature precious.

She demonstrates a passionate appreciation of the environment and a respect for all life. She also invites you to visit her websites:

www.KarenJeanMatskoHood.com
www.KarenJeanMatskoHoodBookstore.com
www.KarenJeanMatskoHoodBlog.com
www.KarensKidsBooks.com

www.HoodFamilyBlog.com
www.HoodFamily.com

Author's Social Media

Friend her on **Facebook**: Karen Jean Matsko Hood Author Fan Page
Please Follow the Author on **Twitter**: @KarenJeanHood
Google Plus Profile: Karen Jean Matsko Hood
Pinterest.com/KarenJMHood

www.ingramcontent.com/pod-product-compliance
Lightning Source LLC
LaVergne TN
LVHW022111080426
835511LV00007B/755